To Die of a Broken Heart...

O.A.

This book is dedicated to the Love of my Life

Wherever you may be...

Love as a Many Splendoured Thing...

There are many different types of Love; and each class structure denotes a certain type of relationship, surounding -- The Feeling of being in Love... Love for a person; Love for an object; Love for his or her God; Love for money; Love for parents; Love for country; and Platonic Love for friends and neighbours, to name a few types of "Love..." However, one thing is for sure, as there are many different facets of the emotion, once obtained, a person will reach a state of Euphoria, when they are in Love. An augmented state, if you will... The act of loving someone and loving something is not the same notion, and might require tapping into different pleasure receptors, but in releasing endorphins (the pleasure hormone) a heightened sense is achieved. Love can be the beginning of something beautiful, or it can be the ending of something tragic. Either way, Love is the real reason we play with fire in our lives, in touching a hot stove, again and again. The desire to be hungry for something more... The idea of acquiring something intangible but Euphoric, as we take chances to heighten our existence...

      Here is a collection of Love Poems, that I have written over the years. Encased are poems touching on the flighting, whimsical, feeling of being in Love, making Love, and being around Love. Recounting former personal relationships, failed and or successful, I have tried to encorporate the entire gamut of the spectrum of experiencing Love from all vantage points. Any circumstantial anecdotes are purely fictious, and any similar references are mere coincidence, personal quips not withstanding. I have changed names and places to protect the memories I have experienced, and the people whom I Love. Please treat this book as a work of entertaining fiction, and not as a biographical look into my personal life... For my personal life is much, much more boring than the heat between these book covers...

O.A.

Poems

To Die of a Broken Heart

Ritenuto

The pain of a ruptured aorta like a volcanic uproar
      searing the insides of a young lover lost in youth
      may seem unbearable once erupted.
But in Molten lava trickling down the mountainside
      reshaping the landscape in its luscious beauty–
      there is a resurrection at the heart of spring.

In breeding lilacs,
The gravest of desires
Feeling the weight of another *Rain Season*
Pain pouring in your heart again...
Pain pouring in your heart again...
Like raindrops collecting at the bottom
      of a dirty windowsill –
Dashing hopes of an early honeymoon
Drowning the crimson colours
Leaving you in solitude;
      there is time for reflection.

The solitude you feel
      is the apogee in every lover's orbit.
The pain is the brief circumvention
      from the gossamer of human connection.
To explain it is a paradox
To feel it is practical
But just mark my words:

Tomorrow as the sun will rise once more
The rooster will crow at dawn
The eagle will take flight beyond the horizon
And as the stars will surely shine
      brighter than the night before:

You will live to love again.

O.A.

Dreams Do Come True

Standing here
Where it all began
Near the park bench
Where I sat a sad sad man
I realize it's been a long time
Since you gave up on me that day
And decided to be on your way
But I just wanted to let you know
Because of you I never gave up
On me and what I wanted to do
I couldn't become a failure now
While you were rising somehow
Enjoying cavier'n the cats Meow
All I'm saying is you bet on "you"
And I bet on me too...

Dreams do come true
They really do...
After years of struggling
Mine started to come true...
Even after being so long in the dark
The world had a lil' change of heart
And gave me a role I could play well
As a writer who left a signature mark

Sitting here
Where it all began
On the piano bench
Where I sat a frustrated man
I realize it's been a long time
Since you gave up on me that day
And decided to be on your way
But I just wanted to let you know
Because of you I never gave up
On me and what I wanted to do
I couldn't become a failure now
While you were rising somehow
Enjoying cavier'n the cats Meow
All I'm saying is you bet on "you"
And I bet on me too...

Dreams do come true
They really do...

After years of struggling
Mine started to come true...
Even after being so long in the dark
The world had a lil' change of heart
And gave me a role I could play well
As a writer who left a signature mark

Dreams do come true
They really do...
After years of struggling
Mine started to come true...

I couldn't become a failure now
While you were rising somehow
Enjoying cavier'n the cats Meow
All I'm saying is you bet on "you"
And I bet on me too...

All I'm saying is you bet on "you"
And I bet on me too...

All I'm saying is you bet on "you"
And I bet on me too...

O.A.

The Dreamer and the Beautiful Dream

For Dr. M.L.K. Jr. and all those who share his vision
Of a Multicoloured, multi-racial,
Multi-national world...

On Capital Hill
At the 'Lincoln Memorial'
You delivered the speech
Of the Century for everyone to see
For everyone to hear your poignant words
For everyone to manifest their own Dreams around yours
Of a Multicoloured, Multi-racial, Multi-national, nonviolent world;
And it is here Dr. Martin Luther King Jr.
Your Dream became something to learn...
Through the media you reached millions at home
And around the world, reciting the words:
'I have a Dream...'
'I have a Dream...'
'I have a Dream...'

...That Blacks and Whites can finally co-exist
That all people of the rainbow can be selfless...
That we as North Americans could do better...
To love ourselves and to protect our neighbours
From injustice and inequality...
These were some of your ideals
That you dreamed,
Of becoming real and finally a reality...
No more Apartheid,
No more clashes with Authority
'Nonviolence' was what you preached at the pulpit
And like Mohandas Ghandi you hoped we would get it...
No more segregation, all young folks attending same schools
From coloured neighbourhoods and white neighborhoods too...

If by chance you could have seen
Your 'Poor People's Campaign'
Finally come into fruition in Washington D.C.
And not been jailed in Birmingham Alabama, unlawfully...
Would you be here celebrating
The fruits of your labour in 2022?
Would there be a time for a 'Beautiful Dream'
Of yours to be realized as an achievable truth?

Or would the Legend you are, roll up his sleeves,
And stare at all of us, and then himself also too
            The Man in the Mirror

And proclaim, that we still have work for us to do
            Brothers & Sisters
Before this 'Beautiful Dream' becomes attainable
            In 2022?

I'd like to think that you would be so happy to hear
About the progress we've made all the way out here
With 'Freedom of Speech' and 'Same Sex Marriages'
It may not be a perfect world, but we are conscious
In trying to emancipate the Earth for what it's worth.

But still, this world needs alot of unconditional work.
And because of you we know what we need to learn.

Dr. Martin Luther King Jr. May your soul rest in peace
Knowing Dreamers have caught the torch you threw
And are parading with your words around the world
Igniting bonfires of tranquility listening to your advice
That even though dark is the transformative night
There is light on the other side of the world
Shining with respect as the Sun and Moon do
In everyone's neighbourhoods, Black or White
And co-existence is the best solution
For everyone to share
A heavenly, divine spotlight
That you helped create,
With your triumphant,
Life...

O.A.

The Musical Creature

Ontop of the highest treetops
In the Amazon rain forests
Sits a male White Bellbird
Singing its heart out
For a female mate
A mile away...

The arresting bird call is made
From far far away at first
Then close-up as rehearsed
To the jade green female
When his back is turned
With a screaming note...

His female love now hides
As he twirls in front of her
Screaming his birdsong
Like a deafening whistle
From a blaring foghorn
And then she is torn...

Should she stay with him
Even though he sings
Horribly like a rooster
At the crack of dawn?
Or should she pretend
She's deaf 'n move on?

These are some questions
Such birds ask themselves
Through mating songs...
However, truly its no use
Because he's NO Marvin Gaye...
Singing: "Let's Get it On..."
          "Let's Get it On..."
          "Let's Get it On..."

O.A.

The Blacktop is Sacred Ground

For the Squads
That ran Hickey Courts
Kits Beach, Bonsor, Winslow
And Cameron Rec Centres
In Vancouver, B.C...
Growing up.

Everytime I step onto these courts
I am reminded of how my parents
Put me in sports for after school activities
To keep me out of trouble at a very young age.

I did not join any gangs,
I did not get into any fights,
Never broke any poor girls hearts,
But I became a decent point guard...
Practising out there in the rain, on the sacred blacktop...

And if it snowed, like it did in Vancouver BC growing up
My squad made sure we sweeped the courts clean now
So we all could at least dribble a little outside somehow...
Before we all had to go inside for a very hot cup of Coco...

Everytime I step onto these courts
I am reminded of how my parents
Put me in sports for after school activities
To keep me out of trouble at a very young age.

The blacktop was sacred ground for all of us
Once we stepped onto these courts over time
We left all our worries and any trouble behind
At least until we finished our basketball game.

Then after my squad won,
The first team to twenty-one,
It was back to the grind...
In other words: 'Real Life...'

O.A.

More to Life...

So you're having a baby...
With the partner you've always wanted
Bought the house of your Dreams
Have your dog or cat on the bed when you sleep
And time is an hourglass away
From being correct again each day
Everything is perfect, what else can you say?
The Lord has been good to you and yours in every way
But then like a wrinkle in time
An inflection in a loved one's voice not right
You realize that something's missing
The Lord decides to test your family's insight
By giving your partner a rare disease
She will have the baby but might not live to hear or see
So then you start to think, why is this happening to me?

There's more to life than what you know...
There's more to life than courage and strength
More to life than humility, hope and masculinity
More to life than being scared, down or serenity
More to life than the whole range of all emotions
That will weigh your heart down
From fluttering high above the clouds
Like a Bluebird soaring FREE in the skies
If you find out your partner will eventually die.
There's more to life than what you know...
You just have to have faith in God's plan...
And not be afraid to explore the unknown
Even if in your perfect life, you end up alone.

O.A.

Ride the Tinted Hurst

There is no tomorrow only today.
Tomorrow does not exist.
        Dante's Inferno proved this.
Ride the tinted hurst
        And do not look back.
There is no tomorrow only today.

Ride the tinted hurst...
        When the switchblade of reason
        is pointing in the wrong direction.

Ride the tinted hurst...
        If the world wants to shut you down
        and won't let you shine
        the way I know you can...

Ride the tinted hurst...
        Only if there is no way out
        and you must prove your worth.

Ride the tinted hurst...
        In the thick of night
        until the crack of dawn.

Ride the tinted hurst...
        When you can't see past the horizon.

Ride the tinted hurst...
        When the man with the crooked cane
        can't think for himself anymore
        and must use your words
        in defense of his own.

Ride the tinted hurst...
        When Mercedes is whispering in your ear
        to rise from the dead
        to claim what is rightfully yours.

Right the tinted hurst...
        And do not look back.
There is no tomorrow...

O.A.

If Love is a Disease, I Don't Want the Cure

In life,
There are 3 people
Who will love you,
Unconditionally:
The person with which you grew up...
The person you will marry at the altar...
And the person with whom you will grow old...
For some lucky people, these 3 types of love
Are mechanically all in 1 person;
If you marry your highschool sweetheart
And do not get divorced,
Or they are your parents with nuturing love
In the beginning of your life,
Then a newfound lover, if you get married.
But then a new lover or companion
Later on in life, with a most stable
Satisfying love because you finally
Know how you want to be appreciated...
Each type is different
Each has its perspectives
Each is all-encompassing
Filled with guardianship,
Filled with lust,
And satisfaction,
Right down to the very end of one's life...
Then the ethereal kind of love we receive,
From beyond the grave is divine in presence...
So, I say this with an open heart and soulful mind,
If Love is a Disease, I Don't Want the Cure...
Because this way in my life, I can experience a Love
That is ultimately pure...

O.A.

A Soldier's Return

For Sarah and all those Ladies awaiting...

Incalzando

Through burning fields of balsam with overcast thunder-filled skies
to the seasonal floods of the Danube River in thigh-high muearth
the man who walks the broken path in the aftermath of war --
psychological, physical, or metaphysical
does the deed for the love his regiment cannot give him
and that is the love of his one
Lady awaiting

Days gone by with nothing said weighs heavy on the mind,
and in the beacon of the sender
now with hopes of lighting the way home in the darkest nights.
If not with scarce words of motivity, then with thoughts of clairvoyance
it should be won
because in the heat of passion this L____ becomes the real battle.
The heart beats torridly on this field.
It is in the mutiny of these arms a victorious soldier can die
on both sides.

The men who line her bedside know nothing of a hero
until tears are bled through inflicted wounds of solidarity
and the uncertainty that follows in a subtle rejection
of not wanting to stay but not really wanting to go --
She is then colder than the man she loves
who is in the compound warmed by paid Hellcats
in an indigo round.

There is a word that undermines "lonely."
I believe it is the word "alone."

She needs to see him uniformed, shapeless, or nascently anew;
know he's out-trod the mountainous skyline
crossed the ocean one wave at a time
to finally lay ruptured, hell-bent,
and knocking at her door...
until this Lady awaiting

is waiting no more.

O.A.

The Boy in a Flower Dress, Girl in Corduroy Pants

Con Spírito

Suddenly, he was as beautiful now
As every other woman in the room.
He slipped into his flower-lit dress
In the changeroom near the front
Of the Valentino Garavani store...
As he stepped out into public view
He twirled and dipped on the spot
Soaking in the bright lights above
Like he was on a Westcoast beach
Suntanning and oiling his skin now
In front of a maniacal fashion-savy
Perverted crowd, chanting outloud
His name as he pranced 'n danced
Around 'n round in a store downtown
Showing off his style to his partner...

Immediately, not having a part of it
She thought that she could do one
Better, so she found a pair of pants
And proceeded to try them on too
In a changeroom in the next booth.
As he pranced 'n danced 'n bowed
She put on her corduroy pants quick
And pulled down her zipper 'n strut
Her stuff like a working class hero
Coming home from a construction
Site with a hard hat and lunch box,
In hand as if she were a beefy man
Out on a break searching for pussy.
Together the two were audacious
And definitely a site for the crowds.

So much so, the owner of the store
Yelled out: "Is this both of your own
Coming out parties? Who wears the
Pants in the relationship 'n family?..."

The two models looked surprised,
And just smiled... And just smiled...

O.A.

The Definition of Love in the 21st Century

1. an intense feeling of deep affection.

"babies fill parents with feelings of love"

Similar:

deep affection

fondness

i.
Love...
What is love?
Is it an apology for enduring genocide at the hands of Faith-healers?
Or 20 billion in currency that cannot heal priceless wounds?
Or is it storming Democracy on a hill, expressing your unwanted opinions?
Or is it knowing that your partner is suffering for their incandescent genitals?
Or feeling the tears of the little girl you rescued from being
Smothered, as the FBI raid another establishment...
Love...
What is love?
Is it the xenophobic fabric woven into a country's people performing
An ethnic cleansing of the nation beside them?
Or is it the hunt for more and more testosterone fueled power
That beckons reasoning?
Or spending more Benjamin Franklins in a casino than a posse
Can handle?

The Hedonism of Love
Is worth noting in all lines and facets
Of this 3 dimensional page...
As my meglomaniacal penmanship debunks the myth that Love
Is something we actually understand in the 21st Century...
For the fickle tangible web of deceit that Love defecates
When it is sitting on its throne, is something we are all caught in
As the world burns of Love all over from forest fires and hurricanes
Earthquakes and volcanoes...
Earthquakes and volcanoes...
Erupting Twister-like in Kentucky
Disrupting communities like a mass shooting
Turned sideways, and blurred out on CCTV...
And then thrown up on MTV for a reaction...

Love...
What is love?
Is it the selfish Capitalistic notion of Billionaires and Poverity-mongers
Trading barbs as to how to end World Hunger?
And not understanding, there will always be suffering, no matter?
Or is it Climate Change threatening our Planet, with Heroes
Like Greta Thunberg, the Real Banshee, wailing,
Sounding the mighty Alarum that the end is fuckin' coming?
Or is it the millions of plastic utensils, and plastic bags
In the Pacific Ocean to the Atlantic, choking sealife,
That keeps us awake all bloody night?

Love...
What is love?
In the 21st Century,
I ask myself this...
I ask myself this...
Where is my heart!!!???
Oliver, You selfish human piece of ____
Why do you think you know about Love?

ii.
Ground Zero
With a plan to reduce carbon emissions by 2040
Smoke stacks will be taxed or taken down aback
Ford F150's will be given a new lease on life supercharged
Everything electric, going to save the planet, with a new start
But yet is it enough?
The Man in the Mirror says, *we still have alot of baggaged stuff*
We still have alot of baggaged stuff
Orphaned SOS kids that need care packages pay only *10 cents*
A day...
Did I fail to mention that the Rich and the Meek to save kids
Only have to spend *10 cents a day!!!???*
Love...
And we think we know how to love...
How to love.

iii.
A Man loves a Man
A Woman loves a Woman
A Man loves a Woman too
A Woman loves a Man true
Same sex relationships are finally shaping with purpose
No more conversion therapy shaming Lovers in loveland

But yet bibles still do not have room for acts of this Love
I will not criticize the Church, but here ask is this really us?
Is this really the human race, giving it all its got?
Love...
What is love?
In the 21st Century?

It used to be a Man loving another Man
Or Woman loving another Woman somehow
Would be shunned like Minorities on the run
From the goverment inside the cities' slums...

But Love...
What is love?
Does the Red Rose bloom for two?
Does it bleed a bloody crimson for just you?
Who and what are we? In this day and age?
Can we save everything that we have failed?

iv.
Love...
What is love?
Is it getting the vaccine for everyone in your household?
So the people you should love will be safe and be okay?
If it is, then why is half the world unvaccinated...
And yelling at our Healthcare workers every day?
Why do we even use the word "Love?"
Like its an excuse to be bittersweet in any way...

As the world turns
And the world burns
As the world turns
And the world burns
I will not criticize our Leaders for not trying enough
For its our Billionaires who people strive to be like...
Money still makes the world go around
And we all want a slice of the good life
To throw away our Starbucks cups now
After ordering a Wet Mocha Venti Latte
And hope some Point Dexter comes in
Into our life and picks up a cup after us
And says, *Mr.? I can get you another one, right away...*

Love...
Who is Love?
Is she your wife or husband who you promised
You would never leave, on any given sunny day?
Is it your children that you know need your love
Each and every way?
Each and every way?
I'm just a concerned human being
I'm just a concerned human being
Nothing more...

Just wondering why I am still living
And what the Hell for?
And what the Hell for?
Nothing more...

v.
Love...
What is love?
In the 21st Century,
I ask myself this...
I ask myself this...
Where is my heart!!!???
Oliver, You selfish human piece of ____
Why do you think you know about Love?
Why do you think...
About Love?

The Scientific World Clock, is nearing 12 O'clock, midnight
Inflation is killing the economy
And in different parts of the world, fuel prices are rising...
And protestors are losing their lives
And the stark contrasts between 1st and 3rd world countries
Are widening...
Budgets aren't being balanced, homeostasis is burnt toast
Homelessness has a new name: "Omni-unemployed..."
And War Veterans are still not being fully compensated
And ignored...
But I am doing my part, even though I loathe myself 'n heart
I pay my union dues, and I choose peace everytime
I walk out my front door.
The Definition of Love in the 21st Century
Might be considered multifaceted
As we continue to explore...

I support my local Legion
I support my local Legion
I support my local Legion
I support my local Legion
In case of War.

vi.
Millennials seem to understand...
Not about love, but not giving up
Gen-Xers don't seem to care well
But generation by generation its a getting tougher than tough
People love their Supercar features more than Mother Nature
And all she has to offer us.
So this world might bust...

So this world might bust...
And if it does,
If it does...
We have to live with it...
We have to live with it...
The Earth is full of love
But the real relationship
Is a refusal to see inside
Each of ourselves...
And be the best we can
In loving ourselves first
And then our neighbour
And world as a fleeting
Last chance...
Before the world we love
Becomes entirely fucked...

Before the world we love
Becomes entirely fucked...

O.A.

Ode to Someone I Used to Love

Agreed, you were too good for me...
I was your Captain and you were lost at sea;
The time spent below deck was priceless
But it just proved we were both selfish.
So, its no wonder you dropped your anchor
Far, far away from me when you left here;
And settled in a small skirmish of a town
Down the Westcoast near Comox Valley...
Now with distance between us, and me drifting
Out to sea again, I am seeing messages
In bottles on fire, floating around my boat
In the harbour washing up like orgami cranes
Setting sail as if someone died yesterday...
I just want to know though, are you over us?
Or is there more you have to say about trust?
Because I am tired of drinking your bottles
Of floating rum, reading how you had no fun
As my lungs burn in flames of the memory
Of someone I used to occassionally love...

O.A.

Goodbyes Are Never Easy

Au Revoir

We were once inseparable
Like two runaway freight trains
Racing to their intersecting Deaths
But we both jumped off the tracks
And collided in the heart of downtown
You on a barstool acting all oh so cool
And me sipping on a Mojito playing pool
    until you told me you were quiting school.

I tried to warn you...
Don't do that to yourself now
But you were dared by the in-crowd
To drop out, and move on down South
You said, you wanted to be in movies, acting
And I said, you should finish your senior year first
In case the world didn't see you as a new James Dean
    but you were adamant in getting great reviews
    and wanted to chase your dreams...

So, down you went
Faster than a Bohemian in a liquor store
Down to Hollywood to try your luck and more
You were the Golden Child of this other countryside
But couldn't stand being made an extra with your smile;
It was a recipe for dissaster, and I saw it a mile away...
I came looking for you, to try and bring you back
    but when I arrived in L.A. I heard you drowned
    in a lake all by yourself, you'd been drinking
    and had no more smiles left to give out...
                to give out...
                to give out...

Goodbyes are never easy...
Especially when you can't read
The lips of the one you love
And kiss their smiling mouth...

O.A.

Lovers of Our Time

Inspired by the lives of Rimbaud and Verlaine

Tutti

If I could drown the Sun forever
In the open mouth of the sea
Then pry back the hands of nature
And let the night roam free
Youth would have their playground
Lovers would have their cover
And there would be a time
For you and me

If the joy of being alive
Was not measured in the amount of spilt tears
But in the amount of bedridden fears
Unleashed through public sympathy
Words would subvert The Action
One shoulder wouldn't support humanity
And there would be a time
For you and me

If the world wasn't so heterosexual
In the eyes of emancipation
And they realized that Love transcends it all
With the will and grace of footsteps over broken glass
Then critics would FEEL their faith
My wife would understand, as would your wife
And there would be a time
For you and me

O.A.

Older Now Wiser

Rubáto

To deny one's youth
before the crooked cane intervenes,
and repercussions of a flat tire occur
from tired legs that have outrun their race
is worth some contemplation.
Train the mind, for it's the last
of these muscles to go:
Athlete or Librarian, no matter.
Fill the head with candid thoughts of books,
or a bread and butter skill
to compensate for the newly-weds of gray hair
that will honeymoon in the comforts of your home
with the potential of producing a now broken smile.

O.A.

A Poetic Aphrodisiac

For CM

Coloratúra

Take me to bed with you in the darkest hours of Love's cruel game
When the wishing well in your downcast heart is full of pennies.
Let the firm grip of a Subaltern Yeoman reaffirm your thwarted hide
To the ping and the par of the utmost chocolate fit for feminine wonders.
To bound and leap in mounds of heaping sorrow to rediscover the faith
In man and his greatest invention of making the beast with two backs
Is the greatest gift any man with valor, honour and noble prurience
Wrongly courting a woman of your magnitude to you could give.
I assure you that once he puts down the pen
We all bare the same sentiments.

Besides, I believe Shakespeare over here...
is taking the OTHER waitress home tonight.

O.A.

Lady Ligeia

Lagrimòso

In the mirror your face appears
Unbidden, yet so clear
    Beaming of a radiance
        That speaks of a tethered *Opium Dream*.
    A pool of memories drown my furtive sighs
As lips babble words of truth.

    From the darkness, your voice I hear
Calling me, haunting me
    With unforgotten vows
        Of a bond etched in lover's suede.
    But with my face in tears again I answer
The blackness, *the figmentum* like a drunken fool:

"I Miss You."

O.A.

My Garden Cat

The way you arch your back
Like a feline with nine lives
Making a purring sound now
When I stroke you downtown
Is a gift for my poetic senses
To enjoy; both ears and eyes
Rejoice at the sight and sound
Of my hands molding you here
Like puddy; a new flower vase
You become in blooming under
Bedsheets, your hard nipples
Sprouting like new rose buds...
Pushing through the flowerbed
To reach for the skyline inside
Raining down on you with warm
Drops of delicious dewdrops...
In your mouth and in your hands
Like a garden cat thirsty for milk.

O.A.

For a.k.a. Vishnoo

April 11, 2002

Melos

Ambition is a pleasant chord in the key of life my friend
It's a pivotal V^6 that allows you to change your scene
Or a pivotal $IV^4/^2$ that sends you into a bridge you've called "Dreams,"
But to transpose an octave up without true intent
Reverts your tune into a funk James Brown would clown.
Modes of classic changes in Lydian or Dorian mode
Seems truly insidious without the verve of one's nerve:
And it is exactly nerve that spurs the words to enhance these changes
In a rewrite of one's melody to another key besides "life."

Then there is my point. The world revolves around you --
Not the other way around.
You are your own leading man, us your supporting cast
You are your melody, we are your harmonies
You always told me you wanted to act, and sing
Well guess what?
You've never left the spotlight,
Open your heart.

O.A.

Alive

09/11/01

You are not dead.
You are not deceased.
You are no fathomless tragedy
Binding our bloodlines –
But now a never-ending chorus engraved in memory
Advocating the greatest cry for freedom
    this world has ever known...

As those responsible have not learned –
The heart of a nation is NO palpable thing.
It cannot be broken, ruptured or torn asunder.
It cannot be touched, or hand-held in the palm of a child
    after a Sunday School session as a desired snow-globe –
For its ventricle pulse of pride will coarse through the veins of every last man
    that has lent a hand in fueling his or her own country's economy, indefinitely...
The sound of this mighty drum; this alarum; has awoken many
Echoing the flapping wings of a countryside filled with a paragon of eagles
    brooding over the devastation of another lost home, talons unsheathed
    gripping this headstone of reality...

Yesterday I was Canadian, proudly defining myself in jest against my neighbours...
    but today –
Today I am a Humanitarian; rigid; tense and advocating that no more blood be shed
    than necessary; co-existence may not be the right answer, but alas it is the best.
Then tomorrow –
When tomorrow comes, after the retribution, I will learn to smile again
For all things unjust will inevitably be brought to an end;
And this is the only prophecy one needs to remember...

Until then:
Let no parasites define their chosen hosts
Let no hosts pay refuge to their parasites
For the sum of their parts is not greater than our whole:
Lest we forget...
Lest we forget...
Lest we forget...

Humanity undivided
    is a beautiful thing.

O.A.

Metamorphosed

For Alice (1911 - 1997...)

You are not dead
You are not deceased
You are no fathomless tragedy
Binding our bloodline –
But you've spurred a touch of envy in me.
I'll accept this muddy mix of sobs and runny make-up,
And even the hollow carcass you've left behind
Like the larva of a butterfly;
The ice-warm feel of your parched flesh against my hand,
And the nonexistence of your puckered kiss
    in this world
But I will not cry anymore –
Death is merely the pupal stage of life.

Out there in the void of time and space,
Somewhere within the pillars of cloud
I know you are making your way...
Cradled on the sweeping Eastwinds
Climbing the opal sky to a better place,
You are floating on the pearly wings of faith
Like a butterfly
Like an angel.

The child you knew, you know again
You have flourished into a Sun-lit frame of mind
You have pushed through the Earth's tarpaulin
    and bloomed,
Bloomed in the misty garden sky;
Beautiful? – you are...
And I am envious.

So I'll accept this quick departure
It was beyond your humble hands...
And I will choke my pride
In mending the broken hearts you've evoked...
But I will not cry anymore.
Not while I know you are loop de looping
    around the stars...

O.A.

Winter Cherry Blossoms in Vancouver

You were always a late bloomer
Like Winter Cherry Blossoms in December
It was like you hit your stride now
Right in the middle of your life so
And it has been beautiful to watch
You bloom like the winter-flowers
Outside in rows around downtown
Each bushel a bright pink of buds
That smell like a fragrant perfume
"Sakura Haruno" and a handful of this love.

You were always a late bloomer
Like Winter Cherry Blossoms in Vancouver
And I love that you have come in
In a season that has Christmas
Because your gift is so priceless
You bloom like the winter-flowers
Outside in rows around downtown
Each bushel a bright pink of buds
That smell like a fragrant perfume
"Sakura Haruno" and a handful of truly you,
Truly you.

O.A.

A Symbolic Red Rose

To me,
A single red rose
Means so much
It means 3 words:
That "I love you"
I want to be true
I want to be one
A one woman kind of guy
Its easy to see in my eyes
With this red rose I will try

To you,
A symbolic red rose
Should mean words
Are being made now
To actions somehow
And everything rests
On the cut of the rose
And how under your nose
Our love looks predisposed
As this is how "LOVE" goes

When love is offered
As a single crimson rose;
When love is offered
As a symbolic red red rose;
The Romantic in me...
Wants you to feel the emotion.

O.A.

The Higher Form of Myself

I have heart, but I don't have Star Power
I can be smart or full of wit, but I don't have it
That thing, that makes people look and stare
And say, there goes that celebrity poet right there
I wonder what he's up to, and who cuts his ol' hair?
Most people may look and stare, but they don't care...
But when I stand in front of them all transformed now
Transcending into the vehicle of the poem that is read
And they see and witness the higher form of myself
The magic they feel is the electricity in the air
The genius of the crowd as they get loud
As I recite my lines from my mouth
And Turn This Mutha Out...
And Turn This Mutha Out...

O.A.

Home is Acceptance

So, after all these years
"I've lived like a bird...
Not knowing where my home is..."
Being rejected like 'The Sugar Man'
After being reported that I was dead...
A writer who had no gusto afficionados
A poet with issues in his soul and head
Still looking for a mentor 'n homestead
Or just a place to lay for a minute in bed
And gather myself before I move onward
To another time and to another mistake;
But maybe as I do all my published books
Will be bootlegged or sold out all around
In another country and will be celebrated
For the reason that I just want to be loved 2...
Like we all do... Like we all do... Like we all do.

O.A.

The Impossible

For My Love

Like tears gathering
On the windowsill of my heart
Its raining down here
Dousing the e/in/ternal flames
Of a dire relationship
Doomed from the very ol' start
But like who believe
In the sun rising in another way
Like those who see
That a tattoo can be removed
And you can design
Yourself on a new canvas again
I believe that one day
I believe that it will rain red roses
For each of the years
I spent away from you, so let it rain
Let it rain...

The Impossible Relationship
The Impossible Love
The Impossible One
The Impossible...
Courage to love...
To love.

O.A.

The Cruelest Thing

The cruelest thing,
Is when the mind wants to...
But the ol' body is not willing...
Like needing an oil 'n filter change
When you need a jump start because
The battery on the ol' Honda is drained...
O' how I miss my youthful days,
When my car getting serviced in the body shop
With its soulful mixtapes turned up, and played
Would never be stood up or unfortunately delayed.

O.A.

The Stigma

For My Reputation
And Yours Too...

I'm dressed in all white
A patient gown, tied up
A guest on the Psych Ward
Again like I was before
In the hospital at which I worked...
I am not crazy, although
When I mention why I...
I was arrested and detained
Tonight, it only seems
That the perspective folks
Have is that I don't belong
Around them because I have a "mental illness..."

I was once Married
I was once a Student in University
I was once a Touring Musician
I was once a Lyricist for 3 Musicals
I was once Captain of my Basketball Team
I was once Captain of my Debate Team
I was once a Normal Human Being

But now The Stigma
The discrimination
Against the thoughts
I keep in my head
Are questionionable
Enough here 'n now
To prevent me from
Living a life without
People constantly
Looking in...

I'm living in a glass cage.

O.A.

I Don't Need an Audience (I Just Need You)

It's okay
Over the years
I've learned I'm an acquired
Kind of taste
No one
Wants to hear
Some of the things I have
To really say

But I don't need an audience now
I don't need a crowd,
To call me out...
I don't need everyone being extra loud
I don't need anyone leaving soon
I don't need an audience
I just need you
I don't need an audience
I just need you

It's okay
Most of the time
I've learned I'm an acquired
Kind of taste
No one
Wants the lines
Some of the things I have
To really say

But I don't need an audience now
I don't need a crowd,
To call me out...
I don't need everyone being extra loud
I don't need anyone leaving soon
I don't need an audience
I just need you
I don't need an audience
I just need you
I don't need an audience
I just need you
I don't need an audience
I just need you

O.A.

The Seafarer on the Horizon

Do not fall in love with the sun
If you touch it, it will burn you
Like a hot stove, stealing fire
Like a volcano erupting again;
But no one told this Seafarer
That his job was to not poke it
The sun, as it passed by angry
Staring at the Seafarer dipping
Down into the ocean's horizon.
So, without reason the Seafarer
Took a tenderhook and poked it
Making his ship fall off the Earth
And into an inferno of molten love.

O.A.

My Heart is on Fire Tonight

You called me yesterday
And I wasn't there for you
So today I went out of my way
To call you to say "I love you..."
And hoped that you'd remain
My number one star in the sky
So every night like a diamond
I can watch you shine bright
I can watch you shine bright

As lovers come and go
I just want you to know
I want to be here tonight
Staring into your eyes...
And kissing your mouth

My heart is on fire tonight
Like cupid set the flames alight
Like I was meant to love you, aright
If you need me now, let me hold you
And let's burn the darkness away
Let's burn the darkness away
Like we were a torchlight
Blazing in the night
Aflame

As lovers come and go
I just want you to know
I want to be here tonight
Staring into your eyes...
And kissing your mouth

My heart is on fire tonight
Like cupid set the flames alight
Like I was meant to love you, aright
If you need me now, let me hold you
And let's burn the darkness away
Let's burn the darkness away
Like we were a torchlight
Blazing in the night
Aflame

O.A.

You Ruined My Life

I used to run marathons
I used to swim for miles
I used to be someone I knew
Until you broke my will to survive
Until I had a failure to thrive...
Now I'm broken and falling apart
I need oxygen for my failing heart
I can't breath around you normally
I take a breath and panic anxiously
Because you did the unthinkable, baby
You ruined my life, what else can I say?

You ruined my life
You left me in the night
Alone, afraid and without lights
In the dark you moved on to new heights
In the dark you moved on to new heights
And it's bittersweet
It's painful to realize
But you ruined my life
But you ruined my life

I used to run long distance
I used to sprint for miles
I used to be someone I knew
Until you broke my will to survive
Until I had a failure to thrive...
Now I'm broken and falling apart
I need oxygen for my failing heart
I can't breath around you normally
I take a breath and panic anxiously
Because you did the unthinkable, baby
You ruined my life, what else can I say?

You ruined my life
You left me in the night
Alone, afraid and without lights
In the dark you moved on to new heights
In the dark you moved on to new heights
And it's bittersweet
It's painful to realize
But you ruined my life
But you ruined my life

Now I'm broken and falling apart
I need oxygen for my failing heart
I can't breath around you normally
I take a breath and panic anxiously
Because you did the unthinkable, baby
You ruined my life, what else can I say?

You ruined my life
You left me in the night
Alone, afraid and without lights
In the dark you moved on to new heights
In the dark you moved on to new heights
And it's bittersweet
It's painful to realize
But you ruined my life
But you ruined my life

O.A.

What Kind of Woman Loves a Man Like That?

I'll tell you...
The same woman who still believes in love
And that this man can sweep her off her feet
Even if he's a no-good-for-nothing scoundrel
Devoted to drinking his bottle of Hennessey
And hitting on her friends at the house party
Because she believes he can CHANGE...
CHANGE for good
CHANGE for better
So she'll write him love letters
And place them beside his bottle of whiskey
Hoping he'll have enough left for her you see
But the saddest part, and moral to this story
Is when a woman believes a man can change
Change for good
Change for better
She won't need to feel healthier
Because his negative vibe won't stifle her inside
And she won't feel the need to stay outside now
Far away from the man she loves unconditional

What Kind of Woman Loves a Man Like That?
The same woman that God sees come back
A million times that tries to change him again
And again and again
But in the end, some men cannot win or change
Because they refuse to grow 'n remain the same.

O.A.

Don't Hang Your Head

For the Influencers

When things are not going right tonight
And your late with the rent or mortgage
And the world won't give you more time
And your lover is moving out of storage
Do yourself a favor, and go easy on you
Nothing is simple in this state of mind
If you can look to God for some advice
If you can ask your neighbour for time
Don't you dare hang your head down Sir!
Don't you dare hang your head down Ma!
Pull yourself together and move foward
Turn on the lights, drink some cold water
Open a window and let some fresh air in
Don't you dare live with regrets you hear?
Don't you dare live with regrets you hear?
Life is a rollercoaster up on the mountain
Flying in every direction defying invention
But every new turn is another way a word
Don't you dare house those angry feelings
Don't you dare house those angry feelings
If things don't work out now as you learned
With one more baby step we can now earn
Our way through the most darkened times
Don't you dare...
Don't you dare...
Hang your head down
Hang your head down
Don't you dare...
Don't you dare...
Hang your head down
Hang your head down
Before you have...
Before you have...
Your fair turn at changing your world
Your fair turn at changing your world

Don't you dare...
Don't you dare...
Hang your head down
Hang your head down

Don't you dare...
Don't you dare...
Hang your head down
Hang your head down
Before you have...
Before you have...
Your fair turn at changing your world
Your fair turn at changing your world

We all could use some help from you
If you still care...
We all could use some light from you
If you wish to share...
We all could use some prayers today
If you're still up there...
If you're still up there...
Don't hang your head
Don't hang your head
Don't you dare...
Don't you dare...

O.A.

The Agony and Defeat

Being rejected is like having your heart broken
A thousand times if you've knocked on doors
Only to see that you're not welcome
Because someone else pitched first
Because someone else pitched first

Eyes wandering around
Rolling up and skybound
The Agony and Defeat
Can't be duplicated or be beat
You look to your left
You look to your right
And then you step off the porch
And end up kicking stones now
Down the empty streets
Down the empty streets

Being rejected is like being on the outside now
Of a million mile joke that has arrived by telephone
And you don't see the butt of it still here
Because you are the reason they stare
Because you are the reason they stare

Eyes wandering around
Rolling up and skybound
The Agony and Defeat
Can't be duplicated or be beat
You look to your left
You look to your right
And then you get off the barstool
And end up kicking stones now
Down the empty streets
Down the empty streets

The Agony and Defeat
Is a worse pain indeed
You may think rejection
Is making you stronger
But in fact it makes you
Accept feeling so weak
That when chance does
Come around you can't... Finally sleep.

You thrash and flash around
Like a salmon finally allowed
To swim upstream to lay eggs
You don't sleep, but you wake
Scrambling to get dressed up
And deliver your presentation

You finally get a joke
You finally aim to sell your own
Brand of who you are...
Brand of who you are...
Brand of who you are...

You're finally a "rejection-hound"
You're finally a "rejection-Superstar..."
Skybound.

O.A.

Orphaned in Love

She was dead in his arms
When he kissed her goodnight
Lightning struck her twice
And he felt her body burn bright
Right in his hands shaking
Love was too much for both'em
He loved her too much here
N' she fainted in the pouring rain
Their connection was filled
With electricity and love affection
They were two light bulbs
Turned all the way up: "120 Watts"

Orphaned in Love
They were both dead upon touch
One was too masculine
And the other was too feminine
Together they were ideal
Like a Romeo and Juliet kind of Love
Like a Romeo and Juliet kind of Love
Like a Romeo and Juliet kind of Love

And when they were photographed
They had a smile, the forensic leads
Told everyone they were soulmates
And in Death they had had the last laugh...

O.A.

Smashing in the Rain...

Thank you for the memories.

When I used to pick you up late from work
With flowers and your favorite rosè wines
Driving out to Spanish Banks now after dark
You sitting on me, me driving so recklessly
We didn't care who saw us or who was there.
We were two young lovers in love so moved
Kindred paths on a collision course me'n you
And then peeling off each other's clothes too
And jumping out of my Chevrolet Cruze to do
The unthinkable, the forbidden, the revelation
We would undress put on a condom' n smash
Smash, smash, smash, smash, smash, smash
Colliding back in forth sexually in pouring rain
Your body next to mine, drinking wine in sands
With nothing but time on our hands, those days
We were explosive, and without a doubt, insane...
Here's to young love like us smashing in the rain...
Here's to young love like us smashing in the rain...
Here's to young love like us smashing in the rain...

O.A.

To Capture Your Hearts

I never have been that good now
At cooking or so capture the flag
But to get some of your attention
Even for a moment I would brag
About how many shoes I do have.

Dance a jig here in a park square
I would light my hair on fire too
And run down the streets naked
Or skydive now out of an airplane
Into a swimming pool in East Van
Steal a waiter's pocketbook good
Serving in a Gastown restaurant.

There'a nothing I wouldn't do...
For extra time, love and to flaunt
My gifts to an audience like you
I may not be much to look at now
I may not be much to look at now
But to capture your hearts I'll do it
I'll get around...
I'll get around...

Like a waiter serving downtown
With one thing on his dirty mind
To make all the customers smile
By bending over, and tying shoes.

There'a nothing I wouldn't do...
For extra time, love and to flaunt
My gifts to an audience like you
I may not be much to look at now
I may not be much to look at now
But to capture your hearts I'll do it
I'll get around...
I'll get around...

O.A.

A House of Love

Two birds nestled in a pine tree
In a nest of branches
In a house of love
During all seasons --
Winter, Spring, Summer and Fall --
Constitutes a bond
That wedlock bears
Even after love runs
Dryer than the drywall
Dryer than a river to a waterfall
In dryest times of all
If one can't recall now
Why it is we got married afterall.

But in a House of Love
Anything goes, as you two grow
As you blossom into budding Buddahs
And become wiser than you know
Wedding bells may have been a calling
But to stay "For Whom the Bell Tolls"
Until the very last day, is how it goes
This is the nature of this "Love-show."

Yes, in a House of Love
Anything goes...

O.A.

Skydiving into Your Soul

Way above the clouds
I am staring like an angel down
Looking into your life
And I'm wanting to help you out
I am up on Cloud 9
And in my life everything is fine
But with you, I know
You could use some help tonight
You could use some help tonight

Some people have guardian angels
Some people make arrangements
To have someone help them out
To have someone help them out

So, I'll be skydiving into your soul
I'll be skydiving into your life now
From Cloud 9, an airplane,
Like thunder rolling for days
When you call my name
I'll be there to help you
In every possible way
In every possible way

Faster than a speeding bullet
Faster than running through it
I will come from the clouds
Like lightning striking down
When you call my name
I'll be there to help you
In every possible way
In every possible way

When you call my name
I'll be there to help you
In every possible way
In every possible way

O.A.

Half of My Heart

I haven't been in love
In a very long long time
I forget what it is like
To have someone on my mind
I forget about signs:
Like trembling knees
Loss of many words
And also getting hurt
But I believe in you so very much
I want to give you this:

"Half of my heart..."
With this beautiful kiss.
And hope we are one of the lucky ones
Who actually make it...

O.A.

Snow Flurries Across the City

As I peer through the window
And watch the snow pile up outside
And I contemplate calling in sick again
And wonder about a winter wonderland
I feel a gust of wind climb inside here
And shake me to my sunken core
As I open my front door to the world
And how I think it all looks so pretty
Snow flurries across the sleeping city
Twinkling lights shining bright covered
In myriads of white snow - snowflakes
And as I yawn, and go back to bed again
I realize how beautiful it is to be awake
And witness the snow blanketing parts
Of an urban landscape, with so much heart
With so much Zambony-ice-driven heart.

O.A.

The Glamour and Glitz

Extravagant displays
Of wedding receptions
Glamourized ways
Of showing affection
But all this means
Nothing in the end
If the world stops turning
And we end up losing friends
If the world stops turning
And we end up losing friends

Time to get our hands dirty
Time to for a climate revolution
Time to get it done before thirty
Time to offer up real solutions

Save all the glamour and the glitz
Before thats all we have in the end
Save all the glamour and the glitz
To when we are past all of this mess
The glamour and the glitz
The glamour and the glitz
Either way we'll finish this...

Superficial games
At working receptions
Glamourized ways
Of showing affection
But all this means
Nothing in the end
If the world stops turning
And we end up losing friends
If the world stops turning
And we end up losing friends

Time to get our hands dirty
Time to for a climate revolution
Time to get it done before thirty
Time to offer up real solutions

Save all the glamour and the glitz
Before thats all we have in the end
Save all the glamour and the glitz

To when we are past all of this mess
The glamour and the glitz
The glamour and the glitz
Either way we'll finish this...

Instrumental:

Save all the glamour and the glitz
Before thats all we have in the end
Save all the glamour and the glitz
To when we are past all of this mess
The glamour and the glitz
The glamour and the glitz
Either way we'll finish this...

The glamour and the glitz
The glamour and the glitz

O.A.

Like Camping Under the Stars

Pitch a tent
And I'll come through
Set a fire pit up
And I'll spend some time
With you
The night is young
And the stars are out
And where you rest
Your head is a new route

Its been so long
Since I've spent
Some time with you
Let me now love you

Like camping under the stars
I just wanna be where you are
I'll set up a fire, we'll go higher
And we'll tell stories after dark
Counting the stars...
Counting the stars...

Roast a log
And I'll come through
Set a fire pit up
And I'll spend some time
With you
The night is young
And the stars are out
And where you eat
Your food is by your mouth

Its been so long
Since I've spent
Some time with you
Let me now love you

Like camping under the stars
I just wanna be where you are
I'll set up a fire, we'll go higher
And we'll tell stories after dark
Counting the stars...

Counting the stars...

In the open air
In our favorite National Park
We'll pitch a tent counting stars
We'll set up a fire, we'll go higher
Being closer to Mother Nature
Being closer to Mother Nature

I'll set up a fire, we'll go higher
And we'll tell stories after dark
Counting the stars...
Counting the stars...

I'll set up a fire, we'll go higher
And we'll tell stories after dark
Counting the stars...
Counting the stars...

O.A.

Dreamscape Lover

I wake up thinking about you
And what it would mean
If we spent more time together
Just you and me
Just you and me
You come into my dreams
A lavishing ravishing being
And I can't help but put you
On a pedestal
And worshipping you too

You are my Dreamscape Lover
And I don't want no one else, no other
You're always on my mind, in my dreams
Because you mean the world to me...
Because you mean the world to me...
Dreamscape Lover
Dreamscape Lover

I keep awake thinking about you
And what it would mean
If we spent more time as lovers
Just you and me
Just you and me
You come into my dreams
A lavishing ravishing being
And I can't help but put you
On a pedestal
And worshipping you too

You are my Dreamscape Lover
And I don't want no one else, no other
You're always on my mind, in my dreams
Because you mean the world to me...
Because you mean the world to me...
Dreamscape Lover
Dreamscape Lover

And no part time or full time lover
And no weekends too I want you
In my dreams everynight of the week
Everynight of the week

I want to spend more time as lovers
Just you and me
Just you and me
Just crawl out of my head
And into my bed, lady lady

You are my Dreamscape Lover
And I don't want no one else, no other
You're always on my mind, in my dreams
Because you mean the world to me...
Because you mean the world to me...
Dreamscape Lover
Dreamscape Lover

Because you mean the world to me...
Because you mean the world to me...
Dreamscape Lover
Dreamscape Lover

O.A.

Blaze Again

Words cannot describe
They way you made me feel
That night you suddenly said goodbye
We were close for awhile
You had my back
And I had yours likewise
We were two wolves
Howling at the moon
And running with the pack
And running with the pack

But sometimes I wish
You hadn't said goodbye
Sometimes I wish now
You were still in my life...

To blaze with you again
Would be a moment my friend
I would cherish it again and again
'Cause the day you left me
I thought our friendship ended...

Taken care of your family
They way we made that deal
And even though you said goodbye
We were close for awhile
You had my back
And I had yours likewise
We were two wolves
Howling at the moon
And running with the pack
And running with the pack

But sometimes I wish
You hadn't said goodbye
Sometimes I wish now
You were still in my life...

To blaze with you again
Would be a moment my friend
I would cherish it again and again
'Cause the day you left me
I thought our friendship ended...

To blaze with you again
Would be a moment my friend
I would cherish it again and again
'Cause the day you left me
I thought our friendship ended...

To blaze with you again
Would be a moment my friend
I would cherish it again and again
'Cause the day you left me
I thought our friendship ended...

'Cause the day you left me
My world collapsed
I had your back
And you had mine too
But in the end
What was I to do?
Except hope that one day soon
Here or in Heaven,
We could Blaze Again...

O.A.

Climate Change Ballad

Hurricanes and earthquakes
Have plagued our lands
Sustaining the environment
Is more than dirty hands
Pulling out weeds
And planting trees
Now more than ever
We see the change in weather
And we wonder what we've done
To anger sweet Mother Nature...
To anger sweet Mother Nature...

Have you seen them?
The smog-polluted streets
Homelessness on the rise
The forsaken look in eyes
Animals losing their homes
Without anywhere to roam
And still our world is so cold
And still our world is so cold
And we wonder what we've done
To anger sweet Mother Nature...
To anger sweet Mother Nature...

Something's gotta change
Within you and within me!!!

Something's gotta change
Within you and within me!!!

Our climate is on the decline
Our ozone has barely survived
Let's change our approach now
Let's open our eyes and our minds
Before its too late
And we regret the mistakes
And we regret the mistakes
We see the change in weather
And we wonder what we've done
To anger sweet Mother Nature...
To anger sweet Mother Nature...

Something's gotta change
Within you and within me!!!

Something's gotta change
Within you and within me!!!

Something's gotta change
Within you and within me!!!

Something's gotta change
Within you and within me!!!

Oh, oh, oh, oh
Ah, ah, ah, ah

Now more than ever
We see the change in weather
And we wonder what we've done
To anger sweet Mother Nature...
To anger sweet Mother Nature...

Now more than ever
We see the change in weather
And we wonder what we've done
To anger sweet Mother Nature...
To anger sweet Mother Nature...

Oh, oh, oh, oh
Ah, ah, ah, ah

O.A.

In the Maze of My Heart

In the labyrinth
Of the deepest darkest parts
I am wandering
Through the maze of my heart
Looking for the answer
To why we fell apart
And I can't find it
I can't remember
Where we started

In the maze of my heart
I am confused about you
I keep trying to find an answer
But I keep running down corridors
That have nothing to do with the truth
Nothing to do with you...
Nothing to do with you...

In the labyrinth
Of the deepest darkest parts
I am running wild
Through the maze of my heart
Looking for the reason
To why we fell apart
And I can't find it
I can't remember
Where we started

In the maze of my heart
I am confused about you
I keep trying to find an answer
But I keep running down corridors
That have nothing to do with the truth
Nothing to do with you...
Nothing to do with you...

And in the puzzle of my life
And in the maze of my heart
I wish you would get off my mind
I wish you would get off my mark
And let me find a way out
A way out of my dark heart...

In the maze of my heart
I am confused about you
I keep trying to find an answer
But I keep running down corridors
That have nothing to do with the truth
Nothing to do with you...
Nothing to do with you...

I keep trying to find an answer
But I keep running down corridors
That have nothing to do with the truth
Nothing to do with you...
Nothing to do with you...

I keep running down corridors
I keep running down corridors
I keep running down corridors

O.A.

Crash and Burn

I wasn't ready for you
But you knew this too
Yet you drove me insane
Changed your face to name
Broke my pleasure to shame
Who was this mistress now?
Who was this bitch you became?

In the shadows we crept
'Till we had nothing left
Then you stole my heart
Then ripped it all apart...

Now I've crashed and burned
Lost everything I loved and earned
And all I wanna do is find you
And blame you for things removed
And all I wanna do is find you
And blame you for things removed
Crash and burn
Crash and burn

I wasn't used to being used
But you knew this too
Yet you drove me insane
Put on lipstick to play
Broke my body to game
Who was this mistress now?
Who was this bitch you became?

In the shadows we crept
'Till we had nothing left
Then you stole my heart
Then ripped it all apart...

Now I've crashed and burned
Lost everything I loved and earned
And all I wanna do is find you
And blame you for things removed
And all I wanna do is find you
And blame you for things removed
Crash and burn
Crash and burn

Now I've crashed and burned
Lost everything I loved and earned
And all I wanna do is find you
And blame you for things removed
And all I wanna do is find you
And blame you for things removed
Crash and burn
Crash and burn

Take your time
'Cause I will find you
I will find you somewhere
Even if you change your hair
I'm coming to even the score, my dear
I'm coming to even the score, my dear
I'm coming to even the score, my dear
I'm coming to even the score, my dear

I don't hate you now, I just want the truth...
Did you really love me? or was I being used?

Crash and burn
Crash and burn
Crash and burn
Crash and burn

O.A.

If You Know These Chords...

Gather round
Pull up a chair, sit down
Open your hearts
Grab a beer, sing a part
Tonight we gonna celebrate
We gonna make the Lord great
By praising his Holy name
By praising his Holy name

So,
If you know these chords
Feel free to sing along now
We going to have a good time
Playing our favorite song 'n smile
If you know these chords
If you know these chords

Settle down
Pull up a chair, stand up
Open your hearts
Grab a beer, give your trust
Tonight we gonna celebrate
We gonna make the Lord great
By praising his Holy name
By praising his Holy name

So,
If you know these chords
Feel free to sing along now
We going to have a good time
Playing our favorite song 'n smile
If you know these chords
If you know these chords

And the music is all there is
There's no monkey buisness
There's no shannigans here
No Tom Foolery...
We're just people who care
We're just people who care
About the Holy Spirit...

Gather round
Pull up a chair, sit down
Open your hearts
Grab a beer, sing a part
Tonight we gonna celebrate
We gonna make the Lord great
By praising his Holy name
By praising his Holy name

So,
If you know these chords
Feel free to sing along now
We going to have a good time
Playing our favorite song 'n smile
If you know these chords
If you know these chords

We going to have a good time
Playing our favorite song 'n smile
If you know these chords
If you know these chords

O.A.

Born and Raised in Canada

A ferry ride to Horseshoe Bay
And then a drive into town
I grew up here in Nanaimo
Where we were home grown
Never thought to live anywhere else
This was home for our family
And myself...

I grew up here in Canada
Born and raised in Montreal
I lived for awhile in Victoria
And wouldn't trade it for anything else

I was born and raised in Canada
The best country in the world
Don't tell me I don't belong here
Different cultures are preferred
We are a melting pot of cultures
We are a mosaic of a future-love
Where everyone gets along...
Where everyone gets along...

A ferry ride from Tsawwassen
And then a drive into town
I grew up here in Nanaimo
Where we were home grown
Never thought to live anywhere else
This was home for our family
And myself...

I grew up here in Canada
Born and raised in Montreal
I lived for awhile in Victoria
And wouldn't trade it for anything else

I was born and raised in Canada
The best country in the world
Don't tell me I don't belong here
Different cultures are preferred
We are a melting pot of cultures
We are a mosaic of a future-love
Where everyone gets along...
Where everyone gets along...

O Canada, I hope you can live
Among the true North strong and free
And understand I am a part of you now
Like you are with me...

I grew up here in Canada
Born and raised in Montreal
I lived for awhile in Victoria
And wouldn't trade it for anything else

I was born and raised in Canada
The best country in the world
Don't tell me I don't belong here
Different cultures are preferred
We are a melting pot of cultures
We are a mosaic of a future-love
Where everyone gets along...
Where everyone gets along...

We are a melting pot of cultures
We are a mosaic of a future-love
Where everyone gets along...
Where everyone gets along...

O.A.

Star-gazer

I see constellations in the sky
I see stars in the field of night
I see the endless display
Of a moment paved

I see comets and falling hearts
I see worlds from where we are
I see the arrogance next
Of a supernova star

But if you see the words on paper
They make much more sense
I am a kind of nuanced Star-gazer
Just don't ask me what's next
The world knows what to expect
I see we don't have much left...
I see we don't have much left...

I know planets and moons will die
I know the world will say goodbye
I know we are so very young
To be taken by the sun

I know stars will explode with time
I know darkness will turn to light
I know we can't protect everyone
You just have to have fun

But if you see the words on paper
They make much more sense
I am a kind of nuanced Star-gazer
Just don't ask me what's next
The world knows what to expect
I see we don't have much left...
I see we don't have much left...

And if we all have to go
One day I hope we see the show
Of a world on its knees
Begging for mercy, mercy please!
Begging for mercy, mercy please!

But if you see the words on paper
They make much more sense
I am a kind of nuanced Star-gazer
Just don't ask me what's next
The world knows what to expect
I see we don't have much left...
I see we don't have much left...

The world knows what to expect
I see we don't have much left...
I see we don't have much left...

O.A.

Listen to Your Graffiti Heart

Its a cruel, cruel joke
To do someone wrong
When you play with a heart
And they end up gone
But at the end of it all
You have to live with yourself
More than anyone else
After the greatest fall...

So, when things come undone
And you need help from someone
And you don't know your part
You don't know where to start
Listen to yout Graffiti Heart...
Listen to yout Graffiti Heart...

Its a cold, cold world
To do something wrong
When you play with someone
And they end up gone
But at the end of it all
You have to live with yourself
More than anyone else
After the greatest fall...

So, when things come undone
And you need help from someone
And you don't know your part
You don't know where to start
Listen to yout Graffiti Heart...
Listen to yout Graffiti Heart...

Listen to your Graffiti Heart
And change the way you think
Welcome everyone under the sun
As a multi-coloured unit...
As a colour-blind system...

So, when things come undone
And you need help from someone
And you don't know your part
You don't know where to start

Don't judge someone too quickly
Don't overplay your dealt cards
Listen to yout Graffiti Heart...
Listen to yout Graffiti Heart...

Don't judge someone too quickly
Don't overplay your dealt cards
Listen to yout Graffiti Heart...
Listen to yout Graffiti Heart...

Don't judge someone too quickly
Don't overplay your dealt cards
Listen to yout Graffiti Heart...
Listen to yout Graffiti Heart...

O.A.

Inspiration is Everywhere

Through the clouds
See your silver lining
Shining down on you
Like a light that's blue
Your inspiration is here
Its all around you now
In a halo circle that's rare...

Inspiration is everywhere
Follow your heart if you dare
Take ahold of your dreams
And walk along the clouds
To where nothing is as seems
To where they believe in hope
To where they believe...
There is love...

Up in the dark skies
See your silver lining
Shining down on you
Like a light that's true
Your inspiration is here
Its all around you now
In a halo circle that's rare...

Inspiration is everywhere
Follow your heart if you dare
Take ahold of your dreams
And walk along the clouds
To where nothing is as seems
To where they believe in hope
To where they believe...
There is love...

And if the feeling persists
Look for love and make a wish
Lightning will strike you again
If you let it...
If you let it...

Inspiration is everywhere
Follow your heart if you dare

Take ahold of your dreams
And walk along the clouds
To where nothing is as seems
To where they believe in hope
To where they believe...
There is love...

Take ahold of your dreams
And walk along the clouds
To where nothing is as seems
To where they believe in hope
To where they believe...
There is love...

O.A.

Tuck You in at Night

Restless, you say to me:
"Turn off the T.V."
Its time for bed anyhow
So you put the remote down
And curl up next to me
The windows are frosted
Still smoke in the chimney
But you know who's the boss
So you oblige me candidly

But if I could tuck you in at night
Turn off the kitchen 'n bedroom lights
And set you off sailing in your dreams
As someone who cares what you need
And make you believe
I will be here for you...
Anytime you need me
I will have done something good
I will have done something good
Tonight...

Undressing, you say to me:
"Come lay next to me"
Its time for bed anyhow
So you put the remote down
And curl up next to me
The windows are frosted
Still smoke in the chimney
But you know who's the boss
So you kiss me, passionately

But if I could tuck you in at night
Turn off the kitchen 'n bedroom lights
And set you off sailing in your dreams
As someone who cares what you need
And make you believe
I will be here for you...
Anytime you need me
I will have done something good
I will have done something good
Tonight...

And if I get this right
You want me to lay down
Next to you tonight
Well I just want to say now
How I feel deep inside
Let me tuck you in tonight
Let me tuck you in...
Let me tuck you in...

But if I could tuck you in at night
Turn off the kitchen 'n bedroom lights
And set you off sailing in your dreams
As someone who cares what you need
And make you believe
I will be here for you...
Anytime you need me
I will have done something good
I will have done something good
Tonight...

Let me tuck you in tonight
Let me sing you a lullaby...
Let me tuck you in tonight
Let me sing you a lullaby...

Fade Out:

O.A.

Don't Be Afraid to Fail

Sometimes we're afraid
To succeed so we except failure
Its not fair or a solution
To those who know us much better
But its easy not to care
Its easy to not care about the future
That's why it has to stop
No one wants to be a 'Beautiful Loser...'

So, anti-up and get back in the game
There's no time to be down or to fail
For every person that succeeds now
There was one who called his name...

In my crystall ball
I see the Walls of Jericho fall
I see the Kingdom of Heaven call
All in the Holy name of the Father
As it is done my sister and brother
And there's no real reason to wonder
These chains on you need to break
Before hurricanes and earthquakes
But in the eye of the mental storm
Don't be afraid to call his name
Don't be afraid to breath in and exhale
Don't be afraid to let it all go...
Don't be afraid to challenge yourself
Don't be afraid to fail...
Don't be afraid...
Don't be afraid...

Sometimes we're down
So to succeed is a greater thing
Its not fair or a solution
To those who know anything
But its easy not to care
Its easy to not care about it raining
That's why it has to stop
No one wants to be 'Forever Losing...'
'Forever Losing...'

So, anti-up and get back in the game
There's no time to be down or to fail
For every person that succeeds now
There was one who called his name...

In my crystall ball
I see the Walls of Jericho fall
I see the Kingdom of Heaven call
All in the Holy name of the Father
As it is done my sister and brother
And there's no real reason to wonder
These chains on you need to break
Before hurricanes and earthquakes
But in the eye of the mental storm
Don't be afraid to call his name
Don't be afraid to breath in and exhale
Don't be afraid to let it all go...
Don't be afraid to challenge yourself
Don't be afraid to fail...
Don't be afraid...
Don't be afraid...

We all need help sometimes
We all need to open our hearts and minds
So to call him by his name
When we are down and struggling to find
The light
The light
Is the best thing we can do
Praying to him each and every night
To put up a good fight...

So, anti-up and get back in the game
There's no time to be down or to fail
For every person that succeeds now
There was one who called his name...

In my crystall ball
I see the Walls of Jericho fall
I see the Kingdom of Heaven call
All in the Holy name of the Father
As it is done my sister and brother
And there's no real reason to wonder

These chains on you need to break
Before hurricanes and earthquakes
But in the eye of the mental storm
Don't be afraid to call his name
Don't be afraid to breath in and exhale
Don't be afraid to let it all go...
Don't be afraid to challenge yourself
Don't be afraid to fail...
Don't be afraid...
Don't be afraid...

O.A.

Heaven's Gates

When I think about it
What happened to us
We were so very young
But we almost lost one
We almost lost someone
That day on the highway
Its all coming back to me
In the most vivid ways
Now in painful memories

We were steps away
From Heaven's Gates
From touching the sky
That day on the highway
We almost died...
We almost died...

When I think of that night
What happened to us
We were so very dumb
But we almost lost one
We almost lost someone
That day on the highway
Its all coming back I see
In the most vivid ways
Now in painful memories

We were steps away
From Heaven's Gates
From touching the sky
That day on the highway
We almost died...
We almost died...

And our world almost came
Crashing down
Around us now
Around us now
Around us now
But we were saved somehow...
Somehow
Somehow

We were steps away
From Heaven's Gates
From touching the sky
That day on the highway
We almost died...
We almost died...

We were steps away
From Heaven's Gates
From touching the sky
That day on the highway
We almost died...
We almost died...

O.A.

Return From Eternity

They say nothing lasts forever
Even when life is fair-weathered
But what do you do when you've
Been over the rainbow and back?
And realize that fabled pot of gold
Is not really real as the story goes...

Will you return from eternity
A broken soul that is now empty?
Will you give up on love again
Before your story finally ends?
Will you say goodbye
Once again?
Will you say goodbye
Now that its ruined?
Its ruined...

They say nothing gets better
Even when life is fair-weathered
But what do you do when you've
Been across the ocean and back?
And realize that fabled City of Gold
Is not really real as the story goes...

Will you return from eternity
A broken soul that is now empty?
Will you give up on love again
Before your story finally ends?
Will you say goodbye
Once again?
Will you say goodbye
Now that its ruined?
Its ruined...

And if you need to say goodbye
If you need to break down and cry
Know that I'll be there for you
No matter what is the truth...
No matter what is the truth...
Nothing lasts forever
Nothing lasts forever
This is tried and true...

So,
Will you return from eternity
A broken soul that is now empty?
Will you give up on love again
Before your story finally ends?
Will you say goodbye
Once again?
Will you say goodbye
Now that its ruined?
Its ruined...

Will you say goodbye
Once again?
Will you say goodbye
Now that its ruined?
Its ruined...

O.A.

A Place in My Heart

To be Canadian
To fall in love again and again
With a crimson country
That has a beauty with no end
Where a pint of beer can be shared
With amazing cultures and friends
Where places like the Grand Prairies
Niagra Falls, Bowen Island and P.E.I.
All have that Canadian beauty that I
Have fallen in love with again and again
Hands down, is the best experience to date...

There's a special place in my heart
For a piece of Canadian landscape
From the Rocky Mountains
To Squamish to 100 Mile House
We are blessed here,
There's no doubt...
We are blessed here,
There's no doubt...

To be honoured
To fall in love again and again
With a crimson paradise
That has a beauty with no end
Where a pint of beer can be shared
With amazing cultures and friends
Where places like the Buchard Gardens
Empress Hotel, Montreal and P.E.I.
All have that Canadian beauty that I
Have fallen in love with again and again
Hands down, is the best experience to date...

There's a special place in my heart
For a piece of Canadian music
From the Tragically Hip, The Arkells
To Gordon Lightfoot to Shania Twain
We are blessed here,
There's no doubt...
We are blessed here,
There's no doubt...

There's a special place in my heart
For a piece of Canadian food
From the Montreal Poutine
To Banff's Beaver Tail to Bagels
We are blessed here,
There's no doubt...
We are blessed here,
There's no doubt...

There's a special place in my heart
For all things produced in Canada
Call me homegrown,
Call me down,
I love to hear the sweetest sounds
Of the Canadian wild,
Outside town,
Its the best country around
Its the best country around
Its the best country around

O.A.

Miscarriage

Met you at our highschool reunion
And you told me you had a crush on me
Spent some time afterwards together
And you asked me to move in with you
One thing lead to another, falling in love
And then you told me you were pregnant
I celebrated with friends and everyone
But I never saw it coming in the distance

I told everyone I was having a son
I told everyone
You were due in June
But little did I know you lost the baby
I told everyone all a little too soon...

We had a miscarriage
We had a return gift from God
We were devestated
And almost gave up on our love
We cried all night and day
The hospital staff stayed
But all we wanted was our child
And we couldn't believe our fate
To this very day...
To this very day...

You were more devastated than me
And you told me you would leave me
Spent some time afterwards together
And you asked me how'd this happen?
One thing lead to another, falling in love
And when you told me you were pregnant
I celebrated with friends and everyone
But I never saw it coming in the distance

I told everyone I was having a son
I told everyone
You were due in June
But little did I know you lost the baby
I told everyone all a little too soon...

We had a miscarriage
We had a return gift from God

We were devestated
And almost gave up on our love
We cried all night and day
The hospital staff stayed
But all we wanted was our child
And we couldn't believe our fate
To this very day...
To this very day...

And I don't know how we made it through
But you were strong and I was strong too
And we never looked back that very day
We just agreed to never bring him up...
Never bring him up again
As we placed him in his grave...

We had a miscarriage
We had a return gift from God
We were devestated
And almost gave up on our love
We cried all night and day
The hospital staff stayed
But all we wanted was our child
And we couldn't believe our fate
To this very day...
To this very day...

But all we wanted was our child
And we couldn't believe our fate
To this very day...
To this very day...

Spoken:
But I still love you
So let's try again
When you're ready
Somehow, someway
We'll have our baby...
We'll have our baby...

O.A.

When Life Got Hard

Quit drinking 6 years ago
Found God again so you know
Fell in love with a woman
And bought a home off a dirt road

These things were fine now
I had my dreams answered somehow
I was the happiest man here
I was the happiest man all around

But then something happened
That rattled my faith in the Lord
The woman I married fell in love
With someone else she got bored

So,
I picked up a bottle, got in the car
And went down to the local gogo bar
And sat there, until my nightmares
Figured out, I was down for the count
Yes, I had a broken heart...
And this is what happened to me...
When life got hard, when life got hard
When life got hard...

Quit gambling 5 years ago
Found God again so you know
Fell in love with a stray dog
And rented a condo as a new home

These things were fine now
I had my dreams answered again now
I was the happiest man here
I was the happiest man all around

But then something happened
That rattled my faith in the Lord
The stray dog I found got hit bad
By someone who drove a 150 Ford

So,
I picked up a bottle, got in the car
And went down to the local gogo bar

And sat there, until my nightmares
Figured out, I was down for the count
Yes, I had a broken heart...
And this is what happened to me...
When life got hard, when life got hard
When life got hard...

But in a flash the woman I loved
Came back, to me after a few years
And the dog I found, rebounded
And we became one big family here
We became one big family here
My heart was filled with tears...
My heart was filled with tears...

So,
I picked up them up, got in the car
And started to drive as a brand new start
And sat there, until my dreams
Figured out, I was going to be around
Yes, God mended my broken heart...
And this is what happened to me...
When life got hard, when life got hard
When life got hard...

I was down and out
But God came around
I was down and out
But God came around

I was down for the count
But God and I figured it out
I was down for the count
But God and I figured it out

O.A.

My Heart Beats For You

Inside my heart
There's a hollow part
Dedicated to housing
Just you and me, baby
And I know its hard
To separate the parts
But I love you truly
Like someone blind
In the candlelight dark

My heart beats for you
Now you know the truth
There's nothing I wouldn't do
You're the Angel I won't lose
My heart beats for you
Like a record skipping a beat
It flutters as if you missed me
You're the song on replay, repeat...

Inside my heart
There's a hollow part
Dedicated to allowing
Just you and me, baby
And I know its hard
To calculate the parts
But I love you truly
Like someone turned on
In a concert after dark

My heart beats for you
Now you know the truth
There's nothing I wouldn't do
You're the Angel I won't lose
My heart beats for you
Like a record skipping a beat
It flutters as if you missed me
You're the song on replay, repeat...

And the world has to know
How much you mean to me
How much you need me
You are the rhythm
To my soul

My heart beats for you
Sometimes out of control...
My heart beats for you
Sometimes out of control...

My heart beats for you
Now you know the truth
There's nothing I wouldn't do
You're the Angel I won't lose
My heart beats for you
Like a record skipping a beat
It flutters as if you missed me
You're the song on replay, repeat...

My heart beats for you
Like a record skipping a beat
It flutters as if you missed me
You're the song on replay, repeat...

O.A.

To Find Universal Love

To find your tribe
To find your ride or die
To find your ride or die
To find Universal Love
To find your group
To find where you fit in
To find where you get in
Is to be sent love from above
Is to be sent love from above

'Cause this world can be cold
It can tear you apart, leaving you alone
It can wear you down, before you get out
But at the end of the day
But at the end of the day
You want to locate, in any way
A group of people who see you
For you...
For you...

To find Universal Love
To find that kind of trust
To be appreciated is a must
To find that magical touch
That is bestowed unto you
From heaven above...
From heaven above...
Through friends who love you
For you...
For you...
Is the greatest thing
You can do
Is the greatest thing
You can do

To find your tribe
To find your ride or die
To find your ride or die
To find Universal Love
To find your group
To find where you fit in
To find where you get in
Is to be sent love from above

Is to be sent love from above

'Cause this world can be cold
It can tear you apart, leaving you alone
It can wear you down, before you get out
But at the end of the day
But at the end of the day
You want to locate, in any way
A group of people who see you
For you...
For you...

To find Universal Love
To find that kind of trust
To be appreciated is a must
To find that magical touch
That is bestowed unto you
From heaven above...
From heaven above...
Through friends who love you
For you...
For you...
Is the greatest thing
You can do
Is the greatest thing
You can do

And once you find that group
Of people who appreciate you
Who have your back, no matter what
You can kick back, and finally relax
'Cause no matter what happens
They will be your tribe throughout life...
They will be your tribe throughout life...

'Cause this world can be cold
It can tear you apart, leaving you alone
It can wear you down, before you get out
But at the end of the day
But at the end of the day
You want to locate, in any way
A group of people who see you
For you...
For you...

To find Universal Love
To find that kind of trust
To be appreciated is a must
To find that magical touch
That is bestowed unto you
From heaven above...
From heaven above...
Through friends who love you
For you...
For you...
Is the greatest thing
You can do
Is the greatest thing
You can do

O.A.

Blessed Reunion

Haven't been on an airplane
Since I took that walk of shame
Back from our 1st reunion 10 years ago
I just want you all to know...
I didn't fit in then, so I won't fit in now
But you have me convinced somehow
That I have to be there...
That I have to be there...
Back in that old town
Back on that Holy ground

I don't see the point
Of inviting me again
But as a favor to you all
I'll come see some friends

But the truth is, ever since she died
I sit in my house, and close my eyes tight
And wish upon the stars at night
That she would come back into my life
That she would come back into my life
Come back into my life...
Come back into my life...

Haven't talked to anyone
Since I took that wreath home
Back from our 1st reunion 10 years ago
I just want you all to know...
I didn't fit in then, so I won't fit in now
But you have me convinced somehow
That I have to be there...
That I have to be there...
Back in that old town
Back on that Holy ground

I don't see the point
Of inviting me again
But as a favor to you all
I'll come see some friends

But the truth is, ever since she died
I sit in my house, and close my eyes tight
And wish upon the stars at night

That she would come back into my life
That she would come back into my life
Come back into my life...
Come back into my life...

And I guess its best
If I don't mope about
But its been so long
Since I've gone out...
Since I've gone out...

I don't see the point
Of inviting me again
But as a favor to you all
I'll come see some friends

But the truth is, ever since she died
I sit in my house, and close my eyes tight
And wish upon the stars at night
That she would come back into my life
That she would come back into my life
Come back into my life...
Come back into my life...

And as I stand here now
Before my blessed reunion
I know I'll see everyone
That knew us from our communion
From the church where we married
I just wish she was one more face
That I would see now in this place...
That I would see now in this place...

Oh, oh, oh...

O.A.

Your Reflection in the Water

As I lose myself in you
And you lose yourself in me too
I can't help think all this time
You have been mine, all mine
And all that I wish for now
Is that we stand the test of time
And you don't go crossing my mind

But when I see you
In the shower of rain
I can't help love you
Each and every day
Each and every day

Its like a lifelong mirror
Your reflection in the water
Your reflection in the rain
The downpour brings us
A brand new life
A brand new day
For us to love each other
Again and again

As I see myself in you
And you see yourself in me too
I can't help think all this time
You have been good, so good
And all that I wish for now
Is that we don't run out of time
And I don't go crossing your mind

But when I see you
In the shower of rain
I can't help love you
Each and every day
Each and every day

Its like a lifelong mirror
Your reflection in the water
Your reflection in the rain
The downpour brings us
A brand new life
A brand new day

For us to love each other
Again and again

And its like I see into your soul
One night you're mine,
Next day I don't wanna let go...
Everytime I see you
I wanna love you
Like you don't know
Even in the rain
Your reflection has a glow...
Your reflection has a glow...

Hey, hey, hey
Hey, hey, hey

Everytime I see you
I wanna love you
Like you don't know
Even in the rain
Your reflection has a glow...
Your reflection has a glow...

O.A.

Phenomenal Eyes

Like windows to the soul
Your eyes open up wide
And lights ebb 'n flow
Through your portal eyes
I see you staring at me
With your beautiful lashes
Winking a million miles
A second, memories crash
Into the world around us
Into the world around us

You have phenomenal eyes
And I cannot hide, I realize
Your hazel pupils, blue iris
Are hard to resist
Are hard to resist
Like temptations for a kiss
Your phenomenal eyes
Are hard to resist...

Like windows to the soul
Your eyes give me a smile
And lights ebb 'n flow
Through your portal eyes
I see you staring at me
Through your windows, baby
Winking a million miles
A second, memories crash
Into the world around us
Into the world around us

You have phenomenal eyes
And I cannot hide, I realize
Your hazel pupils, blue iris
Are hard to resist
Are hard to resist
Like temptations for a kiss
Your phenomenal eyes
Are hard to resist...

And they're a deep swimming pool
Your eyes as I try and keep cool
I would dive right in, but first listen

Will you love me as that look
You have in your eyes?
Or will the light fade from us
Over time, over time?

You have phenomenal eyes
And I cannot hide, I realize
Your hazel pupils, blue iris
Are hard to resist
Are hard to resist
Like temptations for a kiss
Your phenomenal eyes
Are hard to resist...

Like temptations for a kiss
Your phenomenal eyes
Are hard to resist...

O.A.

Long, Long Way From Home

There's a house that sits at the end of this road
A brick house on slabs that I once owned
'Till the mortgage wasn't paid and I had to move
And then that's when you were done with me too

I did everything I possibly could
To get back in your good books
But it was like you wouldn't listen
I was talking to an empty kitchen

Now I'm a long, long way from home
Trying to get back to that old country road
I know things won't be the same now
But I want to finish building that empty house
I want to finish building that empty house
Hoping you'll hear about it,
And come running back home...
And come running back home...

I used to watch the sun set at the end of this road
From a brick house on slabs that I once owned
'Till the mortgage wasn't paid and I had to move
And then that's when you were done with me too

I did everything I possibly could
To get back in your good books
But it was like you wouldn't listen
I was talking to an empty kitchen

Now I'm a long, long way from home
Trying to get back to that old country road
I know things won't be the same now
But I want to finish building that empty house
I want to finish building that empty house
Hoping you'll hear about it,
And come running back home...
And come running back home...

Hoping you'll hear about it,
And come running back home...
And come running back home...

Now I'm a long, long way from home
Trying to get back to that old country road
I know things won't be the same now
But I want to finish building that empty house
I want to finish building that empty house
Hoping you'll hear about it,
And come running back home...
And come running back home...

Hoping you'll hear about it,
And come running back home...
And come running back home...

O.A.

Lord, Lift Me Up

I was once a fool
And didn't believe in you
I was selfish, greedy
Trying to be ever so cool
But then I climbed it
I climbed my life's mountain
And came back down
Like a man who was certain
Like a man who wasn't hurtin'
Anymore...

Tired of the abuse
Tired of the chains
I wish it would rain...
I wish it would rain...
And wash my sins away
And wash my sins away

Lord, lift me up
Take me to higher ground
Lord, raise me up
Lift me off of the ground
Elevate me
Elevate me
I believe in love
I believe in love

Lord, lift my spirits
When I read these holy lines
Lord, raise my spirits
Lift my heart and my mind
Elevate me
Elevate me
I believe in you
I believe in you

I was once so rude
And didn't believe in you
I was cold, and needy
Trying to be ever so cool
But then I climbed it
I climbed my life's mountain
And came back down

Like a man who was certain
Like a man who wasn't hurtin'
Anymore...

Tired of the abuse
Tired of the chains
I wish it would rain...
I wish it would rain...
And wash my sins away
And wash my sins away

Lord, lift me up
Take me to higher ground
Lord, raise me up
Lift me off of the ground
Elevate me
Elevate me
I believe in love
I believe in love

Lord, lift my spirits
When I read these holy lines
Lord, raise my spirits
Lift my heart and my mind
Elevate me
Elevate me
I believe in you
I believe in you

And I believe in you
I believe in miracles
I believe in you so much
And I want you to believe in me
Believe in all of us
Don't abandon me
Don't forlorn any of us
It's in you that we trust...
It's in you that we trust...

Tired of the abuse
Tired of the chains
I wish it would rain...
I wish it would rain...
And wash my sins away
And wash my sins away

Lord, lift me up
Take me to higher ground
Lord, raise me up
Lift me off of the ground
Elevate me
Elevate me
I believe in love
I believe in love

Lord, lift my spirits
When I read these holy lines
Lord, raise my spirits
Lift my heart and my mind
Elevate me
Elevate me
I believe in you
I believe in you... Tonight

O.A.

A Miracle of Faith

Drowning
In your dreams so slow
Then a hand reaches in
And grabs you
And brings you home
Sometimes
When we think we're done
The Lord reaches out
And holds you
And loves you like his son

If you think dreams
Don't come true
I'm here to tell you
I'm here to tell you
That's not true

If you make room
In your heart
For the Holy Ghost
And hold them
Your dreams close
Then one fine day
You'll experience
A miracle of faith
A miracle of faith

Fighting
In your dreams alone
Then a hand reaches in
And grabs you
And brings you home
Sometimes
When we think we're done
The Lord reaches out
And holds you
And loves you like his son

If you think dreams
Don't come true
I'm here to tell you

I'm here to tell you
That's not true

If you make room
In your heart
For the Holy Ghost
And hold them
Your dreams close
Then one fine day
You'll experience
A miracle of faith
A miracle of faith

And they say the Lord works
In mysterious ways
In mysterious ways
So, if your dreams
Keep you awake at night
Then that's alright...
Then that's alright...

He could be making you...
Battle ready...
Battle ready...
To fight for your dreams
To fight for your dreams

O.A.

We are BC Strong...

There's a province
On the Westcoast
Where a smile can get you
Anything you need it to
Where people help each other
Through what they're going through
Filled with great towns
With lush scenery and greenery
And the best fisheries all around

Some people walk on through
Some people stay awhile too
Some people make this a vacation destination
But for me and my community
Its a place we call home
And its easy to see this
And why we call it our own...

Love is where the heart is
And we got alot of heart here!!!
In case you didn't know
We're all Canucks deep down
And Whitecaps too
We're got each others back
In every situation
No need for motivation
Love is where the heart is
And love has been here all along
You see my friend
This isn't the end
But a new beginning
Our world may be changing
But we're still marching on
I am BC Strong...
We are BC Strong...

There's a city or two
On the Westcoast
Where the people will help you
Through anything you need them to
Where people help each other
Through what they're going through

Filled with great communities
With lovable sports teams and dreams
And a wonderful showcase of eateries

Some people walk on through
Some people stay awhile too
Some people make this a vacation destination
But for me and my community
Its a place we call home
And its easy to see this
And why we call it our own...

Love is where the heart is
And we got alot of heart here!!!
In case you didn't know
We're all BC Lions deep down
And Whitecaps too
We're got each others back
In every situation
No need for motivation
Love is where the heart is
And love has been here all along
You see my friend
This isn't the end
But a new beginning
Our world may be changing
But we're still marching on
I am BC Strong...
We are BC Strong...

No floods, no storms
Are going to change the norm
We might have to adapt here
But we'll never change course
We've been living here too long
We've been through alot
But we're still marching on
I am BC Strong...
We are BC Strong...

O.A.

The Greatest Sacrifice

Written by an Ordinary Civilian

I.

The highest distinction
For Military valour and bravery
Is the Poppy Symbol and Sacrifice Medal
Awarded by the Canadian Armed Forces
To a Soldier who sacrificed more
Than their mind, body, heart, and soul
On a battlefield of any kind
Out there in the minefields of everyday life
And with this distinction comes great responsibility
One that very few take lightly
One that very few take lightly
One that very few take lightly

To defend a country
To defend a name
To defend an ideal
Carries a certain weight
Especially, when ordinary folks want you
To defend their honour in your country's name...
And then if you develop PTSD
For simply ordinary people like me
It seems like the world you knew
Is a long long way, and far removed
However, still, Military Veterans Sacrifice
And bleed their country's flag, just the same...
But the honour and distinction is real
One that houses only a few
Brigade and battalion members
In a heirloom of generational fame
In a class of becoming a household name
However, this is not why the few, serve again and again...
Achieving distinctions all across the grain
From what I understand,
Most would serve in silence, without you
Ever knowing their name...
Ever knowing their face...
Ever knowing their sacrifice...
In their own case.

II.
WWI and WWII Veterans
And 1st Responders
Are the real heroes everyday
They sacrifice themselves on their jobs
In everyday life to fight in Battles 'n Wars
They may or may not have started or cared for...
In order to protect the Canadian way
In order to protect the Sovereign faces
In order to protect Women and Children
Its a duty that has not gone unrecognized
Every November 11th we celebrate their lives
We shed tears for those who died
We shed tears for those who died
We shed tears for those who died
And we make sure they do not go unrecognized
Outlining their classifications
Outlining their sacrifices
Reading epitaphs of those loved ones
In graveyard ceremonies of soldiers
Who gave their lives
As we hold the torch high
As we hold the torch high
As we hold the torch high

One foot on Canadian soil
One hand on my chest, as I salute them
I may just be a civilian but I remember
Their sacrifices again and again
I understand why they did what they did
I understand why they do what they do
Because to honour Canada, my homeland
I would serve my country too
I would serve my country too
I would serve my country too
If asked to...

III.
To defend a country
To defend a name
To defend an ideal
Carries a certain weight

Especially, when ordinary folks want you
To defend their honour in your country's name...